Copyrights:

Who are we?

Book Horizon is a publisher based in Winchester, England. In fact, unlike any educational publisher, BH has remained a fundamental tenet of a student's career. And while many current approaches focus on digital content and learning interpretation, they still face serious opposition in the Exam related material success rate. Book Horizon was founded in 2021 by Leon Myers and is now leading this academic institution in Winchester.

Content in this Book:

- Exam Questions & Updated Dumps
- Multiple Choice Questions
- Money Back Passing Guarantee
- Questions at the end for Testing yourself
- Quarterly Manuscript Update for Newer Versions

ANSWER ARE AT THE END OF THE BOOK

QUESTION 1
Which of the following is the best tools for planning, tracking, and reporting time related activities?

A. Gantt Charts

B. Control Charts

C. Histogram

D. Run Chart

QUESTION 2
The External Design Process determines:

A. What are the major components of a product

B. What will happen within each of the major components

C. Provides a map of the sub-components

D. Individual items of sub component

QUESTION 3
The advantage of the Earned Value approach is that it allows the early detection of slippage by using an industry standard approach to:

A. Measure a project's actual progress

B. Forecast both project completion date and final cost

C. Track schedule and budget throughput the project life cycle

D. All of the above

E. None of the above

QUESTION 4
Quality Requirements are generally:

A. Analogue (a range of acceptable values)

B. Binary (on or off, present or not)

C. Either Analogue or Binary

D. None of the above

QUESTION 5
Which function ensures the integrity of the requirements change process?

A. Business Analyst
B. Manager
C. Sponsor
D. Change Control Board

QUESTION 6
Which of the quality factors is a consideration when resources are very expensive?

A. Reusability
B. Flexibility
C. Portability
D. Maintainability

QUESTION 7
Communication tools for the Business Analyst include:

A. Brainstorming
B. Focus Groups
C. Negotiating
D. All of the above
E. None of the above

QUESTION 8
Anything that places a limit on what is possible is a:

A. Requirement
B. Attribute
C. Variable
D. Constraint

QUESTION 9
Pat is documenting the way data will be transformed from an existing system in order to become more compatible with the new system. What type of requirement is he documenting?

A. Quality Requirement
B. Business Requirement
C. Both of the above
D. None of the above

QUESTION 10
A Business Analyst needs to have good communication and interpersonal skills. Example(s) of communication and interpersonal skills include:

A. Listening
B. Interviewing
C. Testing
D. Only A and B
E. A, B, and C

QUESTION 11
Following are the attributes of a good requirement, EXCEPT:

A. Stable
B. Modifiable
C. Ambiguous
D. Traceable

QUESTION 12
Which of the following techniques is used for measuring project performance and progress relative to budget and schedule?

A. PERTs
B. Gantt Chart
C. Earned Value
D. Run Chart

QUESTION 13
The attributes of a good requirement include:

A. Traceable
B. Correct
C. Complete
D. Unambiguous
E. All of the above

QUESTION 14
In an ideal world, the Project Plan and Project Management will be the responsibility of a qualified:

A. Project Manager
B. CIO
C. Quality Assurance Analyst
D. Business Analyst

QUESTION 15
A Requirement is a

A. Generation of a need
B. Specific and detailed statement about what a system must do or be
C. Defined high level functionality of a system

QUESTION 16
Which Use Case convention is used to insert another Use Case that defines an alternative path?

A. Include
B. Extend
C. Exception
D. System

QUESTION 17
For the following scenario which approach is best suited?

Projects where it is difficult to obtain solid requirements due to an unstable environment, especially those in which the requirements will continue to emerge as the product is used.

A. Agile
B. V-Model
C. Prototype
D. Waterfall

QUESTION 18
Continuous Improvement is the definition for Quality proposed by

_____

.

A. Juran
B. Deming
C. Crosby
D. Maslow

QUESTION 19
Which of the following is NOT a Kaizen concept?

A. Quality, not profit, is first
B. Fit to use
C. Defects are a treasure
D. Problem solving is cross-functional and systemic

QUESTION 20
Despite the best efforts to minimize the impact and probability of risk, some risks will always remain. Such risks are called:

A. Operational Risks
B. Residual Risks
C. Business Risks
D. Market Risks

QUESTION 21
Unit Testing generally refers to the testing done by:

A. The business analyst during the requirements phase
B. The developer at the small component level
C. The system tester when testing completed modules
D. The user during acceptance testing

QUESTION 22
The number of participants in JAD sessions are typically higher as compared to other facilitation sessions.

A. True
B. False

QUESTION 23
One of Deming's 14 points is "Work to constantly improve quality and productivity"

A. True
B. False

QUESTION 24
The role of the facilitator is:

A. To help guide a group through a discussion
B. Not be judgmental
C. Create a productive environment
D. All of the above
E. None of the above

QUESTION 25
Which technique is used to reduce the total number of items to a manageable number and to have the resulting items in a priority sequence?

A. Group Ranking
B. Affinity Diagram
C. Brainstorming

QUESTION 26
Reviews and inspections are considered part of testing?

A. True
B. False

QUESTION 27
Which of the following is a tool used for project planning?

A. Delphi technique
B. Peer Review
C. Expected Value Technique
D. Work Breakdown Structure (WBS)

QUESTION 28
Business Event Model is an excellent first step in determining what is to be:

A. True
B. False

QUESTION 29
Suppose a team is developing a web-based ticket distribution system. Which of the following decisions do you think was most likely made during system design?

A. The ticket distributor will include a user interface subsystem
B. The ticket distributor will follow web-accessibility standards
C. The ticket distributor will provide the traveler with on-line help
D. The ticket distributor requirements have been met and satisfy customer needs

QUESTION 30
Reliability is closely correlated with the functional attribute of correctness.

A. True
B. False

QUESTION 31
A Prototype is a:

A. Fully operational representation of a process or system

B. Limited operation representation of a process or system

C. Non-operational representation of a process or system

D. Flow diagram of a process or system

QUESTION 32
Verification is used to determine whether the product meets the requirements as understood by the producer.

A. True
B. False

QUESTION 33
The systematic write-off of an asset over its useful like or some other predefined period is called:

A. Gap Analysis
B. ROA
C. ROI
D. Cash Flow
E. Amortization and Depreciation

QUESTION 34
Which of the following statements about reviews is true?

A. Reviews cannot be performed on user requirements specifications
B. Reviews are the least effective way of testing code
C. Reviews are unlikely to find faults in test plans
D. Reviews should be performed on specifications, code, and test plans

QUESTION 35
The Net Income (Loss) before taxes minus accounting tax effect on income is: _____

A. Income (Gross)
B. Net Income (Loss) before Taxes
C. Income (Loss) from Operations
D. Net Income (Loss)

QUESTION 36

____organizations receive their funding through the collection of taxes, fees and assessments and the sale of properties such as admissions to parks and monuments.

A. For Profit
B. Not for Profit
C. Government
D. Private

QUESTION 37

Poor communication is often the cause of imprecise specifications. In the contracting process, the most critical point where the specifications have the maximum chance for being misinterpreted is:

A. During the planning phase when little is fully understood about the project's requirements
B. The interface between the project team and supplies of services or products
C. During close-out when all parties are attempting to terminate operations and move all assets
D. At meetings and conferences when the agenda limits the subjects to be discussed

QUESTION 38

"Training on the use of new materials" is an example of:

A. Environmental, Competitive, and Regulatory Costs
B. Materials and Supplies Costs
C. Machines, Equipment, and Hardware Costs
D. Methods, Processes, and Procedures Costs

QUESTION 39
Which Six Sigma methodology is used when you are creating new processes?

A. DMAIC

B. DMADV

C. Lean

D. FMEA

QUESTION 40
The diagram is of the:

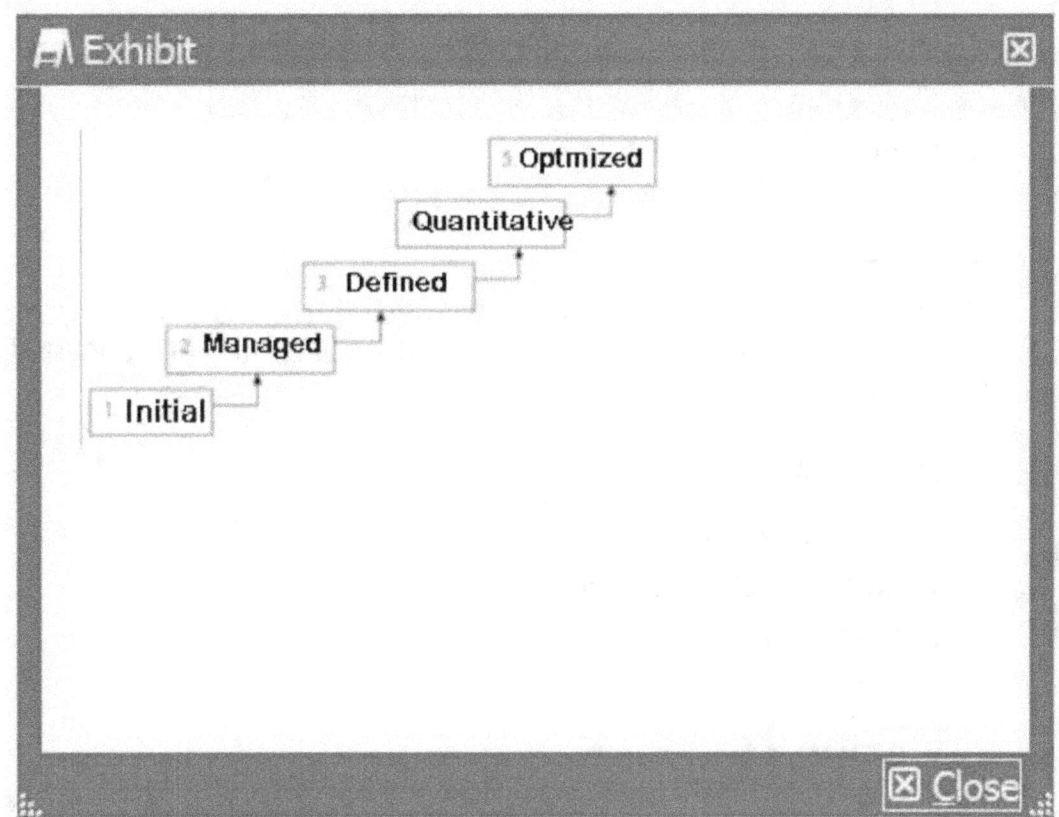

A. ISO 9000

B. Malcolm Balridge Model

C. Capability Maturity Model Integrated

D. Process Workbench

E. None of the above

QUESTION 41
A valid use of an IT measurement program is to record quantitative data that will be used in an employee performance appraisal.

A. True
B. False

QUESTION 42
'Quality is Job One'. This statement could be an example of a

_____.

A. Mission
B. Vision
C. Objective
D. Goal

QUESTION 43
Which document contains the details of the work to be done by a vendor and asks the vendors to submit a bid (or proposal) in response?

A. Project Plan
B. Request for Proposal
C. Statement of Work (SoW)
D. Project Objective

QUESTION 44
Which of the following prescribes a format for Balance Sheets?

A. Business Partner
B. Generally Accepted Accounting Principles (GAAP)
C. Customers
D. Financial Accounting Standards Board (FASB)

QUESTION 45
What ISO standard was introduced to address the issue of Information Technology Service Management?

A. ISO 9000
B. ISO 20000
C. ISO 12207
D. ISO 9001
E. None of the above

QUESTION 46
The work of translating the requirements of what a system must do into a product that will meet those needs is called:

A. Requirements
B. Design
C. Development
D. Prototyping

QUESTION 47
Which of the following is NOT a step of the Vendor Selection Process?

A. Vendor Identification
B. Vendor Selection Matrix
C. Evaluate Performance Criteria
D. Request for Proposal

QUESTION 48
Which of the following is the most important section of a contract?

A. Warranty
B. Parties
C. Deliverability's
D. Penalties

QUESTION 49
Using the "V" Model diagram, what type of testing activity is represented by the letter A?

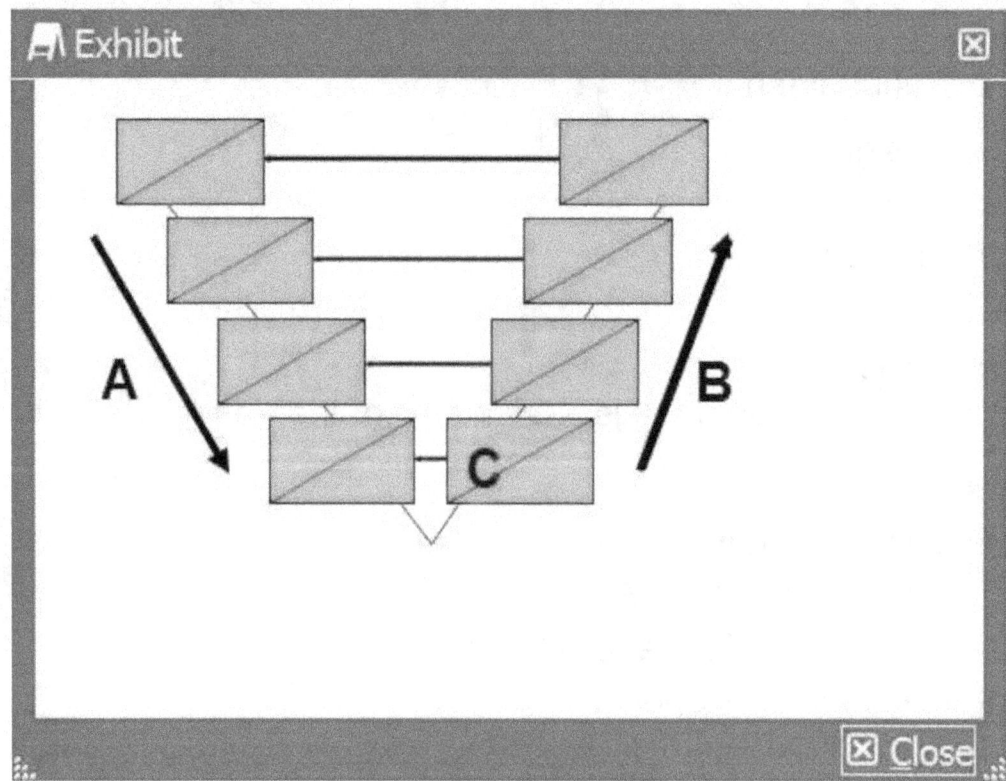

A. Verification or Static
B. Validation or Dynamic
C. White Box
D. Boundary Analysis
E. User Acceptance Testing

QUESTION 50
Internal projects where it is necessary to augment your staff with outside resources would then be considered 'custom software'.

A. True
B. False

QUESTION 51
The primary purpose of Use Acceptance Testing is to verify that the application is ready for production.

A. True
B. False

QUESTION 52
A program validates a numeric field as follows: Values less than 10 are rejected, values between 10 and 21 are accepted, values greater than or equal to 22 are rejected. Which of the following input values covers the MOST boundary values?

A. 9,10,11,22
B. 9,10,21,22
C. 10,11,21,22
D. 10,11,20,21

QUESTION 53
If you acquired COTS software and were attending a demonstration of that software, what aspects of that software would you want to observer during the demonstrations?

A. Understandability
B. Clarity of Communication
C. Functionality of the Software
D. Effectiveness of Help Routines
E. All the above

QUESTION 54
Which of the following is NOT a source of defects in application code?

A. Implementation
B. Requirements
C. Design
D. Coding

QUESTION 55
Performance Based Contracting (PBC) helps:

A. In vendor identification
B. Manage custom developed product
C. All of the products developed by outside individuals
D. Manages the interaction between a software vendor and a requesting organization

QUESTION 56
Which of the following is NOT true?

A. Use case development results in a series of related tests call scenarios
B. Failure scenarios are unsuccessful conclusions that result in the actor abandoning the goal
C. All the scenarios for a single Use Case must meet all of the interactions related to different goal or sub-goal
D. If there is only one path, with no opportunities, changes or errors, there will be no scenarios

QUESTION 57
A hurricane that caused damage to the facility which resulted in many people unable to come to work and thus causing schedule slippage would be an example of a:

A. Common Case
B. Special Cause
C. Any one of the above
D. Both of the above

QUESTION 58
ISO 20000-2 address the issue of ITSM for:

A. Code of Practice for Service Management
B. Specification for Service Management
C. Process Assessment
D. Process Improvement

QUESTION 59
For every organization, the objective is to maximize the resources available for Product Cost by optimizing the resources required or consumed by Appraisal, Prevention, and Failure Costs.

A. True
B. False

QUESTION 60
Fractional Reductions are also referred to as__.

A. Hard Dollars
B. Soft Dollars
C. Actionable Savings
D. Reduced Response Time

QUESTION 61
Which is the following is For Profit Organization?

A. Museums
B. Religious Institutions
C. Charitable Foundations
D. Toyota

QUESTION 62
One of the critical success factors is acquiring COTS software is that the vendor will continue to provide additional features in the future. This critical success factor is commonly referred to as:

A. Ease of Use
B. Expandability
C. Maintainability
D. Transferability
E. Reliability

QUESTION 63
Goals have the following characteristics, EXCEPT:

A. Action
B. Measurable Results
C. Achievable Fast
D. Time Oriented

QUESTION 64
Which of the following is a Level 4 process area?

A. Organizational Process Definition
B. Quantitative Project Management
C. Risk Management
D. Decision Analysis and Resolution

QUESTION 65
FILL BLANK

Briefly explain the different types of funding cycles and explain
their impact on a project.
*Type your answer in the box provided. Use options on the box
tollbar to edit your response as needed before moving to the*

next questions.

ANSWERS

1. Correct Answer: C
2. Correct Answer: A
3. Correct Answer: D
4. Correct Answer: A
5. Correct Answer: D
6. Correct Answer: A
7. Correct Answer: D
8. Correct Answer: D
9. Correct Answer: B
10. Correct Answer: D
11. Correct Answer: C
12. Correct Answer: C
13. Correct Answer: E
14. Correct Answer: A
15. Correct Answer: B
16. Correct Answer: B
17. Correct Answer: A
18. Correct Answer: B
19. Correct Answer: B
20. Correct Answer: B
21. Correct Answer: B
22. Correct Answer: A
23. Correct Answer: A
24. Correct Answer: D
25. Correct Answer: A
26. Correct Answer: A
27. Correct Answer: D
28. Correct Answer: A
29. Correct Answer: A
30. Correct Answer: A
31. Correct Answer: C
32. Correct Answer: A

33. Correct Answer: E
34. Correct Answer: D
35. Correct Answer: D
36. Correct Answer: C
37. Correct Answer: A
38. Correct Answer: D
39. Correct Answer: B
40. Correct Answer: C
41. Correct Answer: B
42. Correct Answer: B
43. Correct Answer: B
44. Correct Answer: B
45. Correct Answer: B
46. Correct Answer: B
47. Correct Answer: C
48. Correct Answer: C
49. Correct Answer: A
50. Correct Answer: B
51. Correct Answer: A
52. Correct Answer: B
53. Correct Answer: E
54. Correct Answer: B
55. Correct Answer: D
56. Correct Answer: C
57. Correct Answer: B
58. Correct Answer: A
59. Correct Answer: A
60. Correct Answer: D
61. Correct Answer: D
62. Correct Answer: B
63. Correct Answer: C
64. Correct Answer: B
65. Correct Answer: See explanation below.
    Explanation/Reference:

Explanation:
There are two interrelated sets of cycles, the accounting cycle, and the industry cycle.
The activities of the Business Analyst are often significantly influenced by the funding cycle of the organization for which they work. Project due dates are often timed to coincide with major revenue periods, or they may be timed to avoid certain other high risk or high activity time periods. Understanding not only how the organization derives revenue (funding sources), but when flows (funding cycles) can help make sense of the apparently senseless and avoid critical mistakes.

www.ingramcontent.com/pod-product-compliance
Lightning Source LLC
Chambersburg PA
CBHW080817220526
45466CB00011BB/3597